How to Manifest
HAPPINESS

How to Manifest Happiness

Your System for Blocking Negativity,
Expanding Positivity And Designing A Happy Life

Logan Chamberlain Ph.D.

Jacquelyn Somach Ph.D.

Book Copyright: ISBN: 978-1-7337564-1-9

Manifesting Happiness, LLC

400 Tamiami Trail South

Venice, FL 34285

Library of Congress Cataloging in Publication date 2-28-2019

Web Site: www.howtomanifesthappiness.com

Dedication

This book is dedicated to all of you that want
to take control of your life and be happier!

Acknowledgements

I want to thank Susan Chamberlain and Jacquelyn Somach for their help designing the cover of this book. They were fun to work with and made significant contributions. I also want to thank my co-author Jacquelyn Somach for all her energy and valuable work on this book. It is rare when two people work so well together and have such great synergy on a project like this. I also want to thank my wife Susan for all her help and support on making this book possible. - Dr Logan Chamberlain

One of the things that make the world a happier place are people who are willing to mentor others. I want to thank my co-author Logan Chamberlain for his mentorship and encouragement, his endless optimism and positivity, and his dedication to helping others experience more happiness. I want to thank my husband, Bill Somach, for his help with editing and for all his patience and support that made writing this book possible. I also want to thank my family and friends for the love and support they provided during this project. - Dr Jacquelyn Somach

Dolphins speak to us of the rhythm of our emotions:

Breathing in joy before plunging into the depths —

And rushing to the surface to do it all over again!

- unknown

Table of Contents

Introduction

The world as we have created it is a process of our thinking.
It cannot be changed without changing our thinking. - Albert Einstein

Happiness is your nature. It is your primary state of being. Manifesting happiness means not only reaching a new level regarding goals and achievements, it means refining and refocusing your mind for strengthening, aligning, and shifting into a richer *experience* of what it means to be alive.

If happiness is a natural way to be, why is it so difficult to maintain? The ways in which we set up our societies, how we live, our environments, our thoughts, beliefs and activities can either support or oppose our ability to sustain our inner balance and vibrancy. How we care for and direct our body, mind, emotions and energies each day directly affects our happiness.

It is often said that happiness is an inside job, or that one must go inward to find happiness. However, in a society that may be opposing happiness more than it is supporting it, going inward isn't enough. Currently the level of negativity is high and it is brought to you more and more rapidly in this quickly evolving age of technology. I realize that a method for manifesting happiness today must address the negativity that is a distraction and in opposition to happiness.

These pages contain a system for successfully manifesting and maintaining happiness even within our current cultural climate. When you apply this system, it acts as a framework for your everyday living that includes practices and techniques for tapping into your natural happy state of being while protecting your positivity from what seems like a constant onslaught of negativity.

I wrote this book because I realize the need for inspiration and a way to stay positive in what seems to be an increasingly negative world. There is too much negativity being brought to our consciousness from a multitude of sources. Too much fake news, bad news and sensationalized information bombarding us every day often causing us to want to escape and challenging our ability to stay hopeful and focused on pursuing our dreams.

We have the capacity to block out negativity both internally and externally and gain control over the effects of our environment on mind and emotions. We can learn to direct our attention solely on that which grows us forward in a positive way. This book provides a system for manifesting and maintaining happiness that can be applied to your daily life.

You will learn how to:

* Block negativity from sources such as negative news, negativity from others, and negative thoughts and self-talk

* Expand positivity in ways such as reprogramming the mind for positivity, strengthening the brain with meditation, and practicing gratitude

* Set goals based on your values and dreams

* Create positive affirmations for making the goals you set a reality

* Design your life with visualization and create a vision book or board

* Put it all together for a daily system of manifesting happiness for life

Much has been written about the power of positivity; however, I know from experience that it takes more than just being positive to design your life and then manifest it into reality. It takes a daily focused effort to control the content that enters the mind. This involves relentlessly rejecting negative thoughts, things, and behaviors and training the mind for visualizing positive situations and evoking positive emotions. It involves disregarding that which you do not want and pointedly focusing only on that which you absolutely do desire. It requires learning the skills of manifesting while accessing the reservoir of positivity that is an innate part of your being.

Today, science confirms our belief in the ability of thoughts to become tangible things. In essence, that which we think, imagine and focus on comes towards us and is achieved. Simply put, we can attract what we desire by putting our attention on it in a certain way. The mind actually does manifest reality. Quantum physics shows us that the vibrational frequency of energy is directly affected by thought because our minds are entangled with the physical universe and, ultimately, the vibrations of our thoughts and words create our world.

This means you already have the ability to tap into your natural inner source of happiness and realize your personal vision of success. However, because you are in a societal environment that has a high amount of negativity, taking control over the quality of information your mind is exposed to is vital. By training your mind you will be able to take command of your thoughts, which affect the reality you are creating for yourself.

Quite simply, we must learn how to block negativity and focus only on positive thoughts and that which we wish to manifest.

The methods offered here provide a way to purposefully direct your mind away from negativity and toward positivity in order to transform the effects of a negative environment on your emotions and your life. The skills you will learn for blocking the many everyday sources of negativity will become daily habits that will give rise to boundless sources of positivity. You will live more in the present moment, your mind aligning with the positive energy of the universe.

With this system you will realize and affirm your goals, reprogram and train your mind, revisit and strengthen your natural inner happy state of being, and bring the precious contents of your dreams into reality. On the whole, you will learn how to manifest the positive outcomes you choose for yourself and bring to light your true blissful nature.

So have a notebook or journal nearby and join me on an adventure to explore, discover and design a life that encourages the innate ecstasy within you that has been upstaged by negativity. Happiness is and has always been yours to manifest. Let me help you remember what you are – powerful and happy!

This book is full of exercises and writing prompts that inspire you to contemplate, express, create and transform. My goal is to teach you how to manifest happiness and to aid you in staying positive despite the negative. Whatever you imagine to be real wealth will be accomplished not by imagining that you will become happy only later after success is achieved, but by experiencing the feeling of happiness and resonating with positivity every day while on your path to fulfilling your dreams - starting now!

Consider that strong, sustainable happiness is achieved on a daily basis. Mastering the skills these pages offer will involve you in a lifelong journey of endless positive growth while creating the life you desire.

Now take action by learning this system and taking control of your life, your future, and your happiness. Come along and let's have an exciting journey!

Chapter One:
Blocking Negativity

If I make dark my countenance,
I shut my life from happier chance.
— Alfred Tennyson, *The Two Voices*

In this first chapter we will discuss the importance of blocking negativity for reducing negative thoughts and making way for positivity. You will be empowered with skills for achieving results that lead to a positive and powerful mindset. You will learn why the first stage in manifesting happiness is to block negative input that causes negative thinking. I will show you how removing negativity such as negative news, negativity from others, and negative thoughts and self-talk will aid you in gaining control of your emotions and will create the opportunity for your mind to focus on positive thoughts that will enable you to manifest your greatest potential for happiness.

It seems that every headline in the news is written to be sensational rather than simply informational. The world news highlights war, terrorism, conflict, earthquakes, the economy, growing unemployment, the falling stock market, violence of any kind, and other global problems.

We now live in a world that's grown so close with instant ways to communicate that it can be quite overwhelming. Just the process of filtering things out can be a huge burden. Add to this the media's slant on reporting negative news by leaving out or marginalizing the positive stories and emphasizing only the thrilling news, and we have a major problem.

Negativity can drown out the positivity that is essential for well-being. We need positivity to imagine, wish, hope, believe, and create. We cannot do this if we are focusing on negativity or being overly exposed to it.

For example, when you are constantly bombarded with negative, sensationalized news, the only thing that gets your attention is news that is even more negative and more sensational. This drives reporters that are looking for what will keep people's attention to search for an ever-increasing level of bad news in the world and to ignore all the good.

This means that what you are receiving on a daily basis is not only a negative story about the world, it's a distorted and inaccurate one. What I mean by "negative news" is bad news that is blown out of proportion and presented in a way that is meant to grab your attention and alarm you. By negative news I do not mean a quick summary of accurate information regarding local and world events. It makes sense to be interested and knowledgeable about what's happening.

Negative news, as often as the media aims for it to reach you, is unhealthy on the psyche and creates negative thinking and negative emotions. I am not proposing that you become reclusive or uninformed but instead that you become keenly aware of what kind of input your mind receives.

Practicing positivity as a skill involves replacing bad thoughts with good thoughts, which changes our emotions from negative to positive. Positivity is experiencing positive emotions, which actually causes changes in the mind and body.

If positivity is good for us why does the media offer an unhealthy serving of negative news 24/7? Unfortunately, it comes down to money being made at the expense of your health and happiness. It's a game being played with an aim to get you addicted to the particular news source in order to expose you to advertising paid for by its sponsors. In order to increase readers, listeners and viewers, the media source gets more outrageous, and by attracting more people, the ad revenues and sales climb. With a strong economic force driving the media and what information we see, making news shocking, gripping, and exciting becomes a priority. This in turn drives us to expect more sensational information, lest we be disappointed and turn elsewhere for our informational fix. And the vicious cycle continues with the news becoming more and more grotesque and inaccurate despite its negative affect on the minds, perspectives, and lives of the public.

This is why eliminating negative input, starting with negative news, is the first stage in manifesting happiness. The mind cannot hold negativity and positivity at the same time. You must remove the negativity and switch your focus for positivity to arise. Quantum physics has shown that thoughts manifest into tangible things. You need positive thoughts to create a positive future.

Even if we are not intending to check the news, it comes at us from every direction from the moment we awake. If we are not conscious of the damage it can do to our mindset, we can be sucked in by labels on news headlines that say MUST READ or YOU NEED TO SEE THIS! However, if we are aware of the big-scary-news-means-money game being played by the media, we can reject it and turn to straightforward informative sources as well as monitor how often we do so.

Thus, the solution to this problem of your mind receiving negative input via negative news being fast-tracked to you throughout your day is to be very selective about what information you allow yourself to pay attention to on a regular basis. You must consciously filter and ignore much of the attention-grabbing headlines and major news stories to avoid getting caught up in the mass hysteria being perpetuated throughout the media.

Negative news becomes negative energy absorbed on a daily basis that is unhealthy and keeps you from focusing on what's most important to you and to the successful achievement of your dreams.

The key is taking the news in small doses from an accurate and balanced source that you can easily manage.

For example, I rarely read the newspaper, watch television, or listen to the radio for news. I choose to use the internet as my main source of news because I can scan the headlines, which allows for the option to choose what I wish to view and limit what I do not want. By doing this I have found I can easily limit exposure to negative news.

It is key here to consider that you truly are 100 percent responsible for your life and how it feels. This is great, though, because being *responsible* means you have the *ability to respond*—the ability to choose a response to anything that is presented to you in life. The formula I like to use to explain this concept is one that Jack Canfield discussed in his book *The Success Principles*. It originates from teachings in Cognitive behavioral therapy. The formula is:

E + R = O (Events + Responses = Outcome)

The key idea is that every outcome (O) you experience in your life—whether it's success or failure, wealth or poverty, wellness or illness, intimacy or alienation, joy or disappointment—is the result of how you have responded (R) to an earlier event (E) in your life. Similarly, if you want to change the results (O) you get in the future, you must change how you respond to events in your life.

Making the choice to respond to negative input by blocking it and refocusing on positive input puts you in control of your mind and your emotions. How you think directly affects how you feel. And how you feel directly affects your perspective and how you function. A negative outlook has you myopically focused on the idea that life is problematic, while a positive outlook broadens your perspective so that you become open, connective, upbeat, optimistic, and solution focused when challenges arise. Positivity provides hope and belief that you can have the happy life you dream about and the inspiration and motivation to take action and manifest that vision into reality.

One of the best ways to change behavior is to monitor it and become aware of what is influencing your thinking. I have some exercises for you to do and I think you'll be amazed by not only how much you are affected by outside sources that you are unaware of on a daily basis but also at how becoming aware of it can empower you with the ability to choose what your mind receives and thus gain control of how you feel. As I mentioned before, our thoughts create our emotions. What we think directly affects how we feel.

Exercise 1: Blocking Negative Sensationalized News Sources and Replacing Them with Neutral or Positive Information

Make a list of all your information sources.

In your notebook or journal record all the sources of news and information that you are affected by every day. Start out with what happens as soon as you arise from sleep in the morning. Are you awakened by the radio alarm? What are the radio disc jockeys talking about? Do you listen to radio or TV while having breakfast or when getting dressed? The aim here is to become more conscious of when you read, listen or watch mass media. Additionally, what are you doing on the computer or phone that may be affecting your thoughts? Considering all the information your mind is exposed to each day, which is negative? Neutral? Positive?

Example:

LIST OF NEWS SOURCES:

- Radio alarm with talk radio station
- MSN browser page
- News apps
- Twitter
- Facebook
- Instagram
- Email subscriptions
- USA Today
- CNN
- FOX
- Gossip

The point of the exercise is to monitor all information sources of negativity that are entering your conscious mind and then block them.

By monitoring, we have the ability to raise our awareness of what our mind is being exposed to and to block incoming negative information that causes harmful programming. Paying attention to negative information leads to negative thoughts, which in turn leads to negative feelings. By eliminating the negative we make way for the positive.

Record all the sources for one week and then review and eliminate all the negative sources and replace them with either neutral or positive sources of information. Some examples of good sources of positive information or positive programming are positive news, neutral sources of news (these provide brief headlines without sensationalized information), self-help, inspirational music, fiction, poetry or other forms of art, learning a new skill, personal and professional development, and biographies.

Monitor yourself after blocking the negative input and see how differently you feel in general, about yourself and about the world around you.

While negative news is a main source of negativity in our high-tech society, there are two other ways negativity arises that are important to consider. These are negativity from others and negativity from self.

Negativity from Others:

It is important to also consider negativity that comes from people in our environment such as gossip and negative attitudes. Whether it is a family member, friend, or co-worker, refrain from joining in with negative conversations or try to transform the conversation by putting a positive spin on it. It is also important to avoid being the one that creates negativity by bringing up subjects such as religion and politics or by sharing a pessimistic perspective that may affect others in a negative way.

How might negativity be reaching you from others? What changes can you make to block this negativity or transform it? Write about this in your notebook or journal.

Negativity from Your Negative Thoughts and Self-Talk

One other way negativity comes at us is through negative self-talk. If you find that you say negative things to yourself in your head throughout the day it is important to be more aware of this, and when it happens, let the thought go and rephrase the situation in a more positive and balanced way or refocus altogether on something positive. The next exercise offers a skill that can help with this. Can you identify any negative thoughts or self-talk that may be having an effect on you? If so, write about this.

Exercise 2: Adopting a Phrase to Say in Your Mind to Counteract the Effects of Negativity

Choose a phrase to say each time you are exposed to negativity such as bad news, violence, a depressing story, unkindness from others, or negative thoughts and self-talk. The phrase can be something like, "I reject this," "Cancel, cancel," or, "I'm envisioning a world that is kind, helpful, and happy." The phrase can become a mantra or affirmation you say each time negativity arises in your environment. Try this for a week every time any form of negativity arises and consider the difference it makes in how you feel.

Exercise 3: Negative to Positive Mindfulness Tool

Sometimes negative thoughts can feel stuck in our mind. The thoughts keep churning around repeating themselves and we feel unable to get them out of our head. We can train our mind so that we gain control over the quality of our thoughts. This exercise provides a skill for doing this.

A strategy to stop negative recurring thoughts is Negative to Positive Mindfulness.

When a negative thought gets stuck in your mind and is affecting your mood in a negative way, you can use the Negative to Positive Mindfulness Tool as a strategy to let go of the thought and produce a positive thought that will improve how you feel. Here's how you do it:

Find your breath—and by this, I mean actually feel where the wind of your breath is on your mouth or nose when breathing a natural breath. Then take the negative thought and visualize it floating away—far away. Then turn your attention back to your breath for just one breath in which you again note the sensation of the wind of your breath. Now you have successfully anchored your mind in the present moment and released the negative thought. From here you can generate a positive thought, which will provide positive feelings. One of the easiest ways to generate a positive thought is to think of something for which you are grateful. As you visualize this, let the positive feeling of gratitude wash over you. Having successfully released the negative thought you can move forward with your day with a positive mind and feeling good.

In this chapter, we looked at how blocking negativity will aid you in gaining control of your emotions and will create the opportunity for your mind to accept the positive thoughts you can generate that will enable you to manifest your greatest potential for happiness. Congratulations on taking this first big step!

Chapter One Summary Points

1. Negativity can drown out the positivity that is essential for well-being.
2. Practicing positivity as a skill involves replacing bad thoughts with good thoughts, which changes our emotions from negative to positive.
3. The mind cannot hold negativity and positivity at the same time. You must remove the negativity and switch your focus for positivity to arise.
4. The key is taking the news in small doses from an accurate and balanced source that you can easily manage.
5. E + R = O (Events + Responses Equals Outcome)- you truly are 100 percent responsible for your life and how it feels.
6. Making the choice to respond to negative input by blocking it and refocusing on positive input puts you in control of your mind and your emotions.
7. Refrain from joining in with negative conversations or try to transform the conversation by putting a positive spin on it.
8. When negative thoughts or negative self-talk arise, let the thought go and rephrase the situation in a more positive and balanced way or refocus altogether on something positive.

Chapter Two:
Expanding Positivity

Keep your face to the sunshine and you cannot see a shadow.

– Helen Keller

In chapter one, we looked at the first step in our system for manifesting happiness—the importance of blocking negativity in order to make way for positivity. In this chapter, we will look at how to take control of your emotions by mastering the practice of blocking negativity and then reprogramming the mind for positivity. You will learn skills for training your mind to experience more positivity within yourself, with others, and in your environment. You will harness the power of your imagination for visualizing a positive future, and you will learn the practices of gratitude and meditation for expanding positivity. By controlling the way you feel you open a direct line to your subconscious and to manifesting your thoughts and beliefs into physical reality.

So often it seems that it is our minds that are in control. The thoughts in our head seem to come and go as they like and it's almost impossible to feel the way we want to feel. The cultural norm is to use caffeine when we are tired, alcohol to relieve stress, and when we can't sleep at night, we take a pill. But instead of continuing to do what society teaches us we can choose to reprogram our mind and take control of our thoughts and emotions.

You really can be completely in control of what you think. I know this may not be common belief. A popular notion is that we are at the mercy of powerful forces that lie outside of us. Thoughts have been programmed into our mind since birth. We have been socialized by family, church and school. Based on our actions since infancy we have received information from the sources in the world around us and from significant others in our world.

Think of yourself as a video recorder that has recorded everything in your surroundings and never erased a thing. It can be a little overwhelming to consider that you have all that information stored in the form of memory. That stored information shapes your thoughts and your actions. It creates perceptual filters that actually block your ability to see and hear information.

I remember in graduate school, I was astounded at the stories related by researchers when performing brain surgery. When specific parts of the brain were stimulated in patients, they would actually relive old situations from their past that were as real and powerful as current experiences. Given these findings, we have a lot of reprogramming to do to overcome any negative biases we have based on these old memories.

Fortunately, a large body of evidence exists showing we are capable of reprogramming our responses to stimuli and it's been proven we can train our minds and change our thoughts.

To be happy and successful we must make a conscious effort to manage and program our thoughts with positivity.

Positivity can be practiced as a skill in response to negativity. Practicing positivity doesn't mean acting cheery when circumstances are bad, but rather it involves experiencing positive emotions that cause changes within the mind and body.

Positivity means being solution focused and replacing bad thoughts with good thoughts, which changes our emotions from negative to positive. When problems arise, it can feel overwhelming. Staying solution focused and looking at the many ways a problem can be solved will take over negative thoughts associated with the situation. Instead of focusing on the idea that there is a problem and what you don't like or don't want, focus on how the situation can be changed or the problem can be solved. Focus on the possibilities, not on what is lacking.

When we treat positivity as a skill and we practice it regularly, challenging times become less painful because our negative perspective is replaced by a more positive outlook. With stress as the leading cause of disease, it is important to recognize that it is brought on by negativity. Positivity has a calming effect that reduces the experience of negative emotions and lowers stress.

As mentioned in chapter one, we know we are 100% responsible for our happiness because E + R = O (Events + Responses = Outcome). The key is our **response** to negativity. We have control because we have the ability to choose how to respond and change the outcome. We can choose to practice positivity as a skill in response to negativity whether it's coming from self, others, or the environment.

Exercise 1: Considering Positivity When Encountering Negativity

When negativity arises, whether from the news, other people, or from your own thoughts or self-talk, ask yourself, *what am I thinking and feeling right now?* Then ask, *what do I want to be thinking and feeling?* Ask yourself the questions, *If I was in a happy state of mind how would I be thinking and how would I be feeling about this situation? How would I be looking at the bright side? How would I be solution focused? In what ways would I be optimistic? How would I find value in this situation?*

Then find something positive to focus on. Focus on this positive thing—it could be something you're grateful for. Feel into how this positive thing makes you feel. You are basically telling your mind, *this is how I'm going to think and feel right now.*

This is teaching your mind that you are in control of thoughts and feelings. This is a skill that can be practiced and mastered. The brain adapts and the mind will learn that you are in charge of what thoughts serve you and what thoughts do not. The mind will become flexible and open to your direction. You will be able to let go of the negative easily and refocus the mind on something positive. In doing so you will be creating good feelings within you at will.

Exercise 2: Envisioning a Positive Day

Envision yourself living out the day thinking in a positive way and feeling the way you want to feel. How do you respond to feeling tired when you wake up in the morning? How do you respond to conflict or something not going your way with work? Imagining yourself living out the day and taking control of your thoughts by focusing on the positive in every situation, and thus controlling how you feel, teaches your mind how it will behave.

Remind yourself regularly, *When I have this or that problem, I will respond in this or that way because I am 100% responsible for my happiness.* You are in charge—not your mind.

Whether negativity is coming from the environment, such as the news or other people, or from your own thoughts or self-talk, it is important to block it and refocus on positivity.

Exercise 3: Positive Words After Blocking Negativity

In Chapter 1, Exercise 2 we discussed utilizing a phrase when negativity arises. This exercise adds to that by offering some specific and powerful words that quickly transform negativity to positivity.

As soon as negativity comes at you in any way, say the words out loud or in your mind, *Delete, delete.* Then follow it up with a positive word, mantra, or affirmation of your choice. I love the word "dolphin" because dolphins are a symbol of happiness and kindness. You could consider saying, *Delete, delete*, and then follow it up with, *dolphin, dolphin*, to turn the mind from negative to positive in an instant. And if saying, *Dolphin, dolphin*, sounds kind of silly then all the better. Keep it fun and positive and watch your thinking and mood brighten up instantaneously!

Exercise 4: Practicing Gratitude

Gratitude is an excellent way of practicing positivity. Thinking of things for which you are thankful not only creates positive feelings within you in the present moment, it also magnifies positive emotions. Practicing gratitude on a regular basis trains your mind to stay focused on what you appreciate, which expands the positivity you experience.

1.To get started, make a list of things for which you are grateful. Now get a jar or a box and label it "Gratitude". Put this list in your Gratitude jar/box. Whenever you think of something you are thankful for add it to this container. At times when you are feeling down, take out some of the notes to remind yourself of what there is to be thankful for.

2.Each morning, imagine three things for which you are grateful. Let the feeling of thankfulness wash over you as you visualize– really feel into the positive emotions that arise.

3.At night, before going to sleep, write down in a gratitude journal three things for which you are grateful. This puts your mind in a positive state before sleeping.

4.Write gratitude letters to people who made a difference in your life. Because you matter, when the recipients of your letters hear from you that you are thankful for how they touched your life, you will have created positivity for them as well as yourself.

5. Look around you, wherever you are (you can do this throughout the day) and look for things or situations you appreciate. When you notice something you do not appreciate, practice ignoring it rather than staying focused on it and judging it as negative. Then redirect your focus to looking for what you do appreciate. This trains your mind to focus only on what you appreciate.

6. Find or purchase a rock that you like. Keep it in a place in your environment where you will see it often. Each time you notice the rock, touch it and think of something for which you are grateful. This keeps the positivity flowing all day!

Exercise 5: Meditation

12 Benefits of Meditation

1. Strengthens your mind
2. Improves your ability to pay attention and stay focused
3. Decreases your capacity to feel emotional and physical pain
4. Broadens your perspective
5. Aids in managing your emotions (anger, aggression, greed, jealousy, fear, anxiety)
6. Training in meditation is about mastering your mind so that you can take control of your emotions and painful thoughts and not be consumed by them
7. Aids you in feeling more emotionally balanced
8. Through meditation you learn that moods, emotions, and negative character traits are temporary and changeable
9. Improves your relationships
10. Increases and deepens your experience of positive emotions such as love, inner peace, confidence, generosity, inspiration, contentment, awe, joy, and altruistic kindness
11. Research has shown that with as few as eight sessions of meditation, meditators rated themselves an average of 20% happier and had improved immune system responsiveness
12. Meditation has been shown to cause an increase in the brain's grey-matter density in parts of the brain associated with memory, compassion, self-awareness, and introspection

Goals of Meditation

- The goal of meditation is to transform the mind from weak to strong. This happens because when we hold our attention in the present moment for extended amounts of time (5 min, 10 min, 20 min, etc.), as we do when we meditate, it strengthens the mind so that we have more control of our thoughts and thus emotions.

- The aim in meditation is to anchor our attention in the present moment through focusing on the breath, and when thoughts arise (or the mind wanders), avoiding judging the thoughts and instead remaining emotionally unattached toward the thoughts, and then letting the thoughts go and gently returning our attention to the breath.

- A big misconception about meditation is that we are supposed to blank out our mind and have no thoughts. However, the goal of meditation is not to have no thoughts, it is to let go of thoughts as they arise and then return our focus to the present moment.

- With meditation we are aiming to train the mind for increased awareness, to remain calm and balanced and to more deeply engage in the present moment.

How to Meditate

Find a quiet comfortable place to sit. It can be in a chair with your feet flat on the ground or on the floor with legs crossed in front.

It helps to keep your spine straight, but your jaw, neck and shoulders relaxed. A good way to do this is to imagine a piece of string pulling you up from the top of your head while all tension leaves the rest of your body.

Your hands can be in a relaxed position on your knees or in your lap. Eyes may be closed or open partially.

Sitting in a state of receptivity with a small smile on your lips, you welcome all inner and outer experiences as they come into your awareness. In this way you are practicing being open and accepting of reality – not judgmental (even if it's a disturbance such as a car horn or dog barking).

Pay attention to the sensation of your breath going in and out of your nostrils. Let your mind rest in the physical sensation of inhalation and then exhalation. You may choose to focus on the rise and fall of your chest or belly. Just breath naturally and be present with your breath.

When your mind wanders, notice the thought with nonjudgmental kindness. Consider that your mind is just doing what it naturally does – shows you pictures. Then gently redirect your attention back to your breath.

If there is a thought that keeps resurfacing or you find it challenging to redirect your attention back to your breath, imagine letting the thought go on a cloud or giving the thought to a friendly dolphin that swims away with it.

Stay with this process of following the breath and letting go of thoughts until it's time to end the meditation.

Try to meditate each day for a minimum of 20 -30 minutes for the greatest benefits. If your time is limited try meditating in small increments throughout your day - 5 minutes here, 10 minutes there, etc.

Exercise 6: Creating Positive Habits

This exercise asks you to start thinking about positivity as part of your daily and weekly plan. We will be building an ultimate plan in Chapter 6. For now, start to consider how practicing positivity can fit into your life for manifesting happiness. Here are three possibilities:

#1. Start the day with a morning practice that gets you focused on positivity and feeling emotionally balanced. This can include body-mind connection practices such as meditation, stretching, yoga, and exercise. Journaling goals and gratitude as well as exposing your mind to positive sources of information that are inspiring and uplifting are some other ways to start your day in a positive way.

#2. Before you go to sleep at night, imagine yourself succeeding in having the happy life you want to have. Imagine yourself thinking the way you want to think and feeling the way you want to feel.

#3. If you know ahead of time that a challenging situation is coming up, then consider rehearsing ahead of time how you will think and feel in the situation.

It is key to understand that our thoughts are what influence the energy that creates our reality. Manifesting happiness is about the forces of energy and the laws of physics. We can tap into the forces of the universe to manifest the life we want.

What happens in your mind is something you can control instead of your mind being in control and life just happening to you. You can take control of your mind by taking control of your thoughts and affecting the energy that creates your reality. You can create the reality you want, the happy life that you want, by utilizing your thoughts as the tools for manifesting.

Wherever you put your focus is where the energy will go. So, wherever you put your thoughts - this is what you manifest. With so many distractions coming at you all day it is important to keep directing your focus in the direction you want. This means staying in the moment by focusing on the breath and then gently redirecting your thoughts on to the positive things and way of living you want to manifest.

In this chapter we explored many ways to expand positivity. In the next two chapters you will be assessing areas of your life to decide what you want to achieve, setting clear goals, and then creating positive affirmations for manifesting your vision into reality.

To change your life circumstances and to realize the successful, happy life you want, you have to do things differently than you are doing them now. Be willing to take the steps to change your lifestyle habits, including the way that you think, and you will be on your way to manifesting your happy life!

Chapter Two Summary Points

1. To be happy and successful we must make a conscious effort to manage and program our thoughts with positivity.
2. Instead of focusing on the idea that there is a problem and what you don't like or don't want, focus on how the situation can be changed or the problem can be solved.
3. The key is our ***response*** to negativity. We have control because we have the ability to choose how to respond and change the outcome.
4. When you focus on something positive you are teaching your mind that you are in control of your thoughts and feelings.
5. Consider saying, "Delete, delete," and then follow it up with, "dolphin, dolphin," to turn the mind from negative to positive in an instant.
6. Practicing gratitude on a regular basis trains your mind to stay focused on what you appreciate, which expands the positivity you experience.
7. Meditation has been shown to cause an increase in the brain's grey-matter density in parts of the brain associated with memory, compassion, self-awareness, and introspection
8. It is key to make practicing positivity part of your daily and weekly plan.

Chapter Three: Setting Goals

Our goals can only be reached through a vehicle of a plan,
in which we must fervently believe, and upon which we must vigorously act.
There is no other route to success. – Pablo Picasso

In the first two chapters we addressed how to block negativity that impedes happiness and how to expand positivity that facilitates it. In this chapter we will explore the power of goal-setting for designing and manifesting your happy life.

If you want to go somewhere, doesn't it help to know how to get where you're going? And doesn't it help for you to locate directions and decide on the best route to take? And if you get lost, do you just stop and find out where you are or do you stop, get help and reconsider a new way to continue on your journey?

Goals are essential for manifesting happiness. Setting goals and actively pursuing them motivates you, gives your life direction, and brings a sense of accomplishment and satisfaction when you achieve them. Happiness doesn't have to be only the end result of realized goals. It can arise as soon as you step onto the path of thinking, planning, and pursuing goals that are important and meaningful to you. Creating goals and pursuing them daily is the way you can transform your values and dreams into a reality.

Life is a journey. Sometimes we get lost along the way. At times we need to stop and reassess, and at other times we want to quit whatever it is we are doing and start all over – just go back to the beginning and start from scratch. Ultimately, the journey continues as destination after destination is reached. The movement and growth towards these destinations and the intermediate stops along the way are what goal setting and planning are all about.

I have set goals for myself for over forty years. I have achieved most of them and I have a fresh set of them currently in place. The bottom line is: if you aren't growing, you're dying, and I'm not ready to cash it in yet. There's a saying I like that emphasizes the importance of having a plan. It is: *People don't plan to fail, they fail to plan*. If we expect to get where we want – or to feel the way we want to feel – we need a well-thought-out plan. That plan must include all the steps needed to reach our goals.

Many authors have written about goal setting and some wonderful programs have been created to help us set goals. I have taken from those programs and added my own unique components to make my own custom program that I'll share with you now.

The only time I have gotten into trouble is when I didn't have a plan and a set of goals.

A lot has been written about making sure your goals are in line with your values. I completely agree and, given that, I also agree that it's challenging to identify all your values. The next exercise offers an effective way to determine your values. Before we do that let's make sure we are all working on the same definition of what values are in our lives.

Values are defined by Webster's dictionary as "the social principles, goals or standards held or accepted by an individual, class, or society," and, "to place a certain estimate of worth on in a scale of values i.e. (to value health above wealth)."

A person's values are learned from many experiences and come from many sources. That's why everyone has a different set of values and that's why it is so vital to understand your values and what drives you before you can set your goals. For example, if you value health as a priority, you are going to set some strong guidelines about what you eat and drink. You may also put exercise as a high priority.

Exercise 1: Value Identification

Let's spend some time identifying our values which will make the goal-setting process much more powerful. You may find you have current values as well as ideal values. Take a look at the following list.

Freedom	Safety
Friends	Security
Family	Confidence
Career	Relaxation
Church	Religion
School	Relationships
Education	Charity
Action	Communication
Fitness	Privacy
Health	Community
Country	Sports
Associations	Clubs
Love	Learning
Travel	

Consider each idea separately and explore your beliefs related to that concept as it pertains to your life. Take some time to write about your beliefs and what you value most. What are your beliefs regarding each of these areas? How much importance and priority do you assign to each area? How do you value each area currently? How would you value each area ideally? What do you envision in each of these areas for creating your most happy life?

Now let's look at eight areas of life that affect our wellness. They are:

- Spiritual-Expanding our sense of purpose and meaning in life. Connecting to the source of enlightenment.

- Financial-Increasing your satisfaction with current and future financial plans for more prosperity.

- Physical-Recognizing the importance of diet and exercise for your health and wellness.

- Emotional-Coping with life and its challenges and creating satisfying relationships.

- Environmental-The need to create a happy place to live in that supports your health and wellbeing.

- Occupational-Gaining personal satisfaction and financial rewards from your work and career.

- Social- Developing a sense of connection to your relationships and belonging to a well-developed support system.

- Intellectual-Recognizing your strengths and finding ways to increase your knowledge and skills.

We have created a great visual to clarify the relationship between the variables: the wellness wheel.

The Wellness Wheel

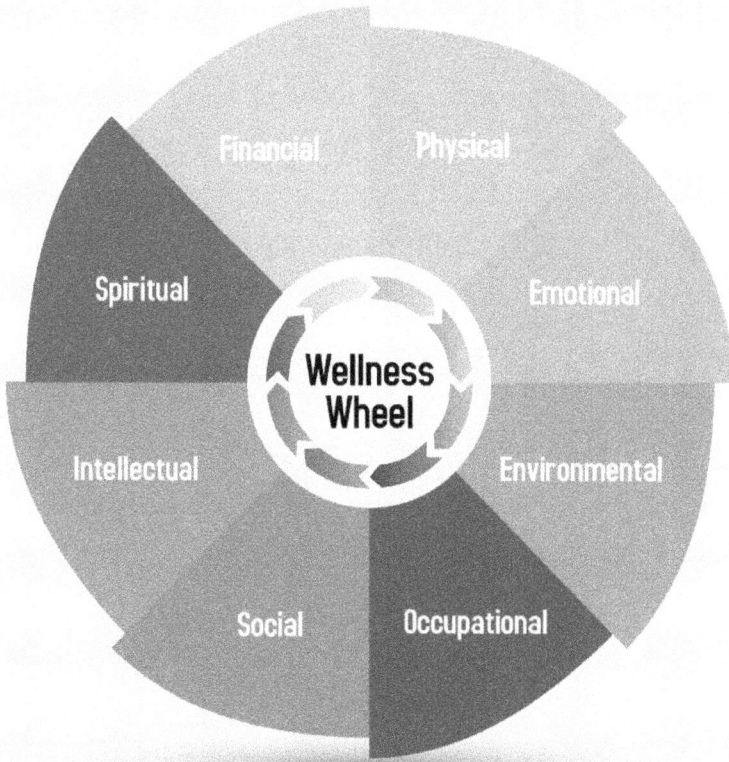

Financial

Physical

Spiritual

Emotional

Wellness Wheel

Intellectual

Environmental

Social

Occupational

Now consider your values and beliefs in each of the eight wellness areas of your life. Rate your happiness from 1–10 in each of the eight areas. This will provide you with a guide to areas that you want to improve and give you tangible things to focus on achieving.

Here is an example of goal-oriented activities in each wellness area that takes into consideration values and beliefs:

Spiritual – Perform a morning meditation for 20 minutes

Financial – Open an IRA and contribute monthly

Physical – Go for 30-minute walk daily and do 15 minutes of weight bearing exercises

Emotional – Make a weekly date with your significant other

Environment – Create a goal to find a new home that better fits your needs

Occupational – Develop a better relationship with your supervisor at work

Social – Strengthen your personal relationships

Intellectual – Read a new book every month that adds knowledge to your passion

In the next exercise, let's take one of the categories above and develop a goal to achieve your desired outcome.

We will use the practice of setting SMART Goals when setting all of our goals.

SMART is a mnemonic acronym, giving standards to guide in the setting of objectives, for example in project management, employee-performance management and personal development. The letters S and M usually mean **specific** and **measurable**. Possibly the most common version has the remaining letters referring to **achievable, relevant** and

time-bound. However, the term's inventor had a slightly different version and the letters have meant different things to different authors, as described below. Additional letters have been added by some authors.

The first-known use of the term occurs in the November 1981 issue of *Management Review* by George T. Doran. The principal advantage of SMART objectives is that they are easier to understand and to know when they have been done. SMART criteria are commonly associated with Peter Drucker's management by objectives concept.

Exercise 2: Setting a SMART Goal

SMART Goal: Specific, Measurable, Achievable, Relevant and Time-bound

Example:

I will set an alarm for 5:30 AM and wake up 30 minutes early each morning starting tomorrow morning, February 21, 2019. I will dress in comfortable clothes and sit in a quiet place and meditate for 20 minutes. After meditation, I will read and focus on my current goals and affirmations before starting my day.

Practice by writing down one SMART goal for yourself.

Once the goal is set, we must make it real. We must write it down and read it every morning and every evening before we go to sleep. We must visualize it, create a picture of it and post it where we can see it every day. Share the goal with a friend and concentrate on the feelings and emotions of achieving it. I recently had a goal of selling a condo that I owned. I printed out a copy of the listing and wrote *sold* across it and put it on my refrigerator in my kitchen. I saw it daily and focused on the sale. It sold in three weeks for a good price!

Begin to consider and write down goals for each of the eight wellness areas of your life. We will be expanding on this in a later chapter, but you can begin to consider these goals now.

Staying positive with negativity around means setting goals to stay focused on no matter what. The aim is to avoid letting negativity cause hopelessness or even acceptance of mediocrity. It's important to create goals that aim for what you really want—not for just okay or for what you are willing to settle for, but for what will truly excite and inspire you!

Planning your life instead of letting it happen to you is key. Staying focused on what you want by creating a crystal-clear vision, and most importantly experiencing the feelings that vision evokes, will let the law of attraction work to your benefit. Creating your life your way and realizing your greatest potential for happiness requires determination and effort. This leads to a discussion of balance.

Balance is an important part of thriving, but to excel at anything we have to be willing to feel out of balance at times.

There are many facets of life and maintaining balance is one of them – especially emotional balance. However, at times we have to focus most of our energy in one area in order to excel or achieve what we consider to be great. This means being willing to move outside our comfort zone into a place that feels new, unstable, and even unbalanced. This is where growth happens and it takes being brave.

It is important to practice taking action toward your goals even with fear. Bravery, confidence, and belief that you can change your circumstances and have the successful and happy life you want is essential.

The greater danger for most of us isn't that our aim is too high and we miss it, but that it is too low, and we reach it. – Michelangelo

You have learned how to block negativity from the outside and the inside, you have learned how to focus your mind on positivity for manifesting your desires, and you have learned how to create goals that will design your happy life. In the next chapter you will learn about creating positive affirmations for transforming your goals from dreams to reality.

Chapter Three: Setting Goals

The power of your beliefs, believing in yourself and believing you will accomplish your goals and create the reality you want will manifest the happy life you envision!

Chapter Three Summary Points

1. Goals are essential for manifesting happiness.
2. If we expect to get where we want – and to feel the way we want to feel – we need a well-thought-out plan. That plan must include all the steps needed to reach our goals.
3. Rating your happiness from 1–10 in each of the eight wellness areas of your life will provide you with a guide to areas that you want to improve and give you tangible things to focus on achieving.
4. SMART Goal: Specific, Measurable, Achievable, Relevant and Time-bound
5. The power of your beliefs, believing in yourself and believing you will accomplish your goals and create the reality you want, will manifest the happy life you envision!

Chapter Four:
Creating Affirmations

Belief consists in accepting the affirmations of the soul; unbelief, in denying them.

– Ralph Waldo Emerson

In this chapter, we will delve into what positive affirmations are and how they work. You will gain skills for using positive affirmations in your life and examples of effective positive affirmations will be provided. You will also learn how to create your own positive affirmations for all of your goals to manifest your vision of a happy life into reality.

What is a Positive Affirmation?

A positive affirmation is a statement that is said often or repeated several times in a row, not only to encourage you as you are speaking it but also to modify your assumptions and beliefs about yourself and the world and to reprogram your mind for manifesting a desired reality.

A positive affirmation acts as a command to the brain that describes your desire as if it is already occurring, as if it already exists, so that your brain immediately begins adapting and working to ready you for this way of being now.

Affirmations work in a powerful way in the brain. There are three important components that define a positive affirmation.

The First Component of a Positive Affirmation:

A positive affirmation is made up of only positive words. For example, *I won't accept being treated unkindly*, is a good idea and worthy quote; however, it is not a positive affirmation because it contains negative words like *won't*. It also states what you don't want and, since thoughts become things, we don't want to affirm, or create, what we don't want.

Even if we are saying we don't want it, denying it still affirms the existence of it. Thus, we want to avoid repeating words that we don't want to manifest into reality. So how could we get what we want out of this statement by reworking it into a positive affirmation? We could say, *I am always treated kindly by everyone wherever I go*. This is a positive affirmation because it contains only positive words.

Positive affirmations that contain only positive words instruct the brain to connect and strengthen the neural connections that prepare the mind and body for the positive reality you are desiring.

The Second Component of a Positive Affirmation:

A positive affirmation is always stated in the present tense. This is because a positive affirmation is stated as if the content of it, the desired state, already exists. Using words like, *I plan to*, or, *I will*, places the desired reality as something for the future rather than a statement of belief that it currently exists.

Statements made in the present tense have the greatest effect in the brain because the brain will adapt to what is stated as presently true. The brain does not take a statement and tuck it aside for future manifestation. It takes what is stated at face value, one word at a time, and immediately gets to work adapting to that which is described by the positive affirmation.

The brain begins creating and strengthening neural connections for readying the mind and body for living that reality. For example, *I will meet the love of my life*, is not a positive affirmation because it is stated as if it is something that will be done at some point in the future. Saying this as a positive affirmation could be, *I am attracting the love of my life, and my life is filled with joy and love.*

The brain interprets this as what is happening currently and adapts to that idea or belief. It is important to stay in the present tense even if this is not the current state in which you are living because repeating this positive affirmation teaches the brain to adapt and become a brain that experiences this state of being now.

When positive affirmations are stated in the present tense, the brain gets to work becoming that sort of brain with those sorts of thoughts that then manifest into things that support your desired reality.

The Third Component of a Positive Affirmation:

A positive affirmation is stated as a fact. Rather than using words like *may* or *might*, positive affirmations use words like *is* and *am*. For example, rather than statements such as, *I may exercise daily*, or, *I might have more abundance in my life soon*, positive affirmations would say, *My life is one in which I exercise daily and have boundless health and well-being*, and, *I am living a life of great abundance and joy.*

In this way the brain interprets the statement as something definite and acts on the command accordingly rather than considering it as only a possibility and so not something to adapt to now. Positive affirmations are like taking your brain to the gym and conditioning the brain and mind with instructions for what areas need to be stronger. We don't tell the brain what it might need to strengthen but what it definitely needs to strengthen now. This way the brain goes to work strengthening the neural connections that support the description of reality stated by the positive affirmation.

This makes positive affirmations an important process in manifesting. You say the positive affirmation over and over and your brain takes it as truth, which causes it to continue to strengthen the neural pathways that prime your mind and body for living the very reality your positive affirmation describes. With positive affirmations stated as fact, everything about you becomes ready and intended toward the manifestation of your desires.

How Positive Affirmations Work:

We can use positive affirmations to change our thinking and change our life. To do this it helps to understand how positive affirmations work in the brain.

Your subconscious mind can be compared to the hard drive of a computer. Like a computer, it can get jumbled up with bad programming from sources such as negative input from your environment, negative self-talk, damaging health habits, and too much stress.

Positive affirmations are suggestions you make to your subconscious mind that transform your thinking patterns. In this way positive affirmations are a way to reprogram your mind the way that you would reprogram a computer. You can remove the old clutter of bad programming, your negative beliefs that are currently creating a less than desirable reality, and produce positive beliefs that can replace the old negative ones and manifest the reality you do desire.

Positive affirmations can be thought of as commands or instructions the brain receives and then processes by firing the neural connections to prepare you for the action that would immediately follow the command. For example, if you say, *I will perform well tomorrow at the recital,* your brain applies the words said to the immediate moment and prepares you in that moment for a good performance, which would not be effective if you are aiming for the next day at the recital. Whereas, *I am always a great performer,* will strengthen neural connections for feeling prepared and confident whenever you perform.

The brain listens to each word individually and applies it immediately. For example, repeating, *I am not sad,* over and over again will not be an effective positive affirmation for avoiding sadness because even though you have the word *not* in front of the word *sad* the brain is still exposed to the word *sad* over and over again. Thus, the brain gets to work immediately preparing you for the action of being sad. An effective positive affirmation for avoiding feeling sad might be something like, *I am filled with joy,* because it is present tense and has only positive words.

And you have commanded your brain to do something rather than not to do something. You have given your brain specific instructions it can work on immediately.

The brain listens to each word individually and applies it immediately.

This is also why it is important for positive affirmations to be stated as truth. The brain will not take as well to a suggested possibility but instead understands a clear stated fact it can get to work on in that very moment. And because the brain is constantly strengthening its connections whenever you feel, act, and do things, it's important to repeat positive affirmations daily. Repeating positive affirmations is powerful because your brain strengthens the connections, reprogramming the mind every time you say the words.

This process of providing daily repeated verbal instructions to the brain that the brain can take literally as a command to be executed immediately in order to prepare you right now for a new reality is how positive affirmations work for manifesting more happiness in your life.

How to Use Positive Affirmations:

1. While you can say positive affirmations any time of day as well as many times a day, it is most important to say them when you are in the alpha brainwave state. This is because the subconscious mind is most open to receiving suggestions while in the alpha state. The alpha state is occurring in the brain as you are waking up in the morning and when you are falling asleep at night. The alpha brainwave state also occurs during prayer and meditation. Therefore, it can be helpful to repeat your positive affirmations at a time when your brain is in this alpha state. This means practicing positive affirmations immediately upon waking, during the day as part of meditation and/or prayer, and before going to sleep at night once you are calm and relaxed.

2. Begin by breathing slowly and deeply three times in and out to the count of 10 while paying attention to your breath. This mindful practice focuses your attention in the present moment and prepares your mind to be alert and open in the now.

3. Repeat the positive affirmations slowly, focusing on what each word means.

4. Experience the positive feelings that arise from envisioning living the reality of the positive affirmation. Sense the uplifting feelings that materialize as you imagine the positive affirmation as true and actually happening right now in your present life.

Examples of Positive Affirmations for each of the Eight Wellness Areas of Life:

Spiritual: I am so happy and grateful that I am meditating every day!

Financial: Money comes easily and frequently to me.

Physical: I am so proud that I am working out three times a week.

Emotional: I will always pursue Happiness and Joy.

Environmental: I have a peaceful place in my home to relax.

Occupational: I love my job and my company.

Social: I am happy and in love.

Intellectual: I enjoy reading new books and learning new things.

Exercise 1: Creating Your Own Positive Affirmations

Begin making a list of positive affirmations that go with each of the goals you are creating in the eight wellness areas of your life. Make sure each of your affirmations contain all three components that define an effective positive affirmation. You will be expanding on this in Chapter Six, but you can begin now.

Exercise 2: Saying and Writing Your Positive Affirmations

Say your positive affirmations out loud to yourself when your brain is in an alpha state such as in the morning when you first wake up, while meditating or praying, and at night before falling asleep. It is also helpful to write down each positive affirmation at least once daily in your journal.

Think big and have fun creating your positive affirmations and believe they will manifest happiness for you! You are on your way!

Chapter Four Summary Points:

1. Affirmations work in a powerful way in the brain. In this way they are different from an inspirational quote.
2. A positive affirmation is made up of only positive words.
3. A positive affirmation is always stated in the present tense.
4. A positive affirmation is stated as a fact.
5. This process of providing daily repeated verbal instructions to the brain that the brain can take literally as a command to be executed immediately in order to prepare you right now for a new reality is how positive affirmations work for manifesting more happiness in your life.
6. While you can say positive affirmations any time of day as well as many times a day, it is most important to say them when you are in the alpha brainwave state.

Chapter Five:
Designing Your Life

What you imagine you create. – Buddha

This chapter is about designing your life to be the happiest it can be. I have provided a walk through a day with tips, skills, and practices for blocking negativity and expanding positivity to provide a strong foundation for staying focused on your goals, tapping into your natural happy state of being, and maintaining inner joy even when negativity arises. Take what you have learned so far from the first four chapters and as you walk through a day with me, apply what you have learned to create your day your way and design what you envision to be your happy life!

Starting Off Your Day

Starting your day off right is the single most important thing you can do to ensure that you will have a happy day. I like to get up early and have some quiet time to reflect and be grateful for what I have accomplished. I have a special place in my home where I can write, read or work on my computer. I like to spend my mornings programming myself and planning my day.

Having a morning plan or practice connects your goals and values to your thoughts and actions for a great start to your day. When your behavior isn't in line with your values for health, abundance, relationships, and career, you can end up feeling less than optimal. For example, you may value having a positive relationship with your partner; however, if you find yourself becoming impatient with them it could be that you are reacting to your environment based on negative habits from the past that have become the default program in your brain.

Having a morning plan or practice connects your goals and values to your thoughts and actions for a great start to your day.

Neuroscientist Joe Dispenza explains that this happens in the brain in response to the environment because the end result of any experience you have is an emotion, and emotionally intense negative experiences make the strongest memories. The brain uses information from the negative memories to create beliefs about the world. These beliefs then go on to create your negative habits.

Every time you learn something, new connections are created in the brain. Your memory maintains these connections via repetition. Thus, the goal as we start each day is to have a plan that includes practices that reprogram the brain with positivity that is strong enough to override the negative beliefs and habits created from what occurred in the past.

In your morning practice you will:

1. Create new and positive experiences that will create new connections in your brain.
2. Make these new experiences emotional so your brain remembers them.
3. Utilize repetition so these new and positive connections become strong sustainable memories that then become the new default for the brain in responding to your environment as you go about your day.

In this way, your morning practice provides daily conditioning and reprogramming for your brain so that old negative patterns will be replaced as new stronger positive patterns are created based on what you really desire.

I adopted an idea from the teachings of Anthony Robbins. He recommends an *hour of power*. In that hour I focus on four things:

Note: Even if you don't have an hour to dedicate to these four practices you can still create an excellent and planned morning practice.

1.   **Positive Programming.**

There are things we can do to feel good emotionally and to create positive feelings about our day. As we discussed in our first two chapters, we need to eliminate negative input and introduce positive thoughts into our mind for positive programming. One thing I do to accomplish this is read some inspiring literature. I offer a list of some of my favorite inspirational books in the appendix.

2.   **Expressing Gratitude.**

I make a list of things that I am grateful for in my life. I have created a master list and I keep adding to it as I have new things I'm grateful for every day. Everyone has things in their life to be grateful for and it's really a wonderful exercise to list them and be thankful for them. Read your list and express your gratitude for each and everything you have listed. Choose ways to practice gratitude from the examples given in the Gratitude Exercise from Chapter Two. Get emotional and associate true feelings of gratitude.

People have said that things are so bad they can find nothing to be grateful for in their current life. I'm sorry, but that is just not true. You can start with the basics such as, *I'm alive this morning.* There are people in the world who count that as something for which to be thankful. You might be grateful that you had a place to sleep last night and some warm clothes to wear. Everyone's life is different and everyone has things that they can be grateful for that are specific to their current life experiences no matter how challenging.

3.   **Reviewing and Visualizing Goals and Affirmations.**

I review my written goals and affirmations and visualize the attainment of each one individually. There is immense power in this activity. Be sure and associate the pride and emotion you feel by obtaining each goal. Imagine that you have already achieved the goal and state of mind you desire.

It's best to read your goals and affirmations out loud and feel the vibrations of the words as you speak them. It is also ideal to visualize your affirmations and goals and include a vivid sensual experience in doing so. For example, see all the goals in the present tense and in vivid color. Pay attention to your feelings and all the other senses associated with the goal or affirmation. Feel a sense of joy and pride in having achieved them and be grateful that the universe has helped you along the way.

You will be learning how to create a vision book or board in Chapter Six that will aid your visualizations and affirmations.

As an expert in creating instant change, Anthony Robbins recommends practicing an *incantation* when doing your affirmations. This is moving your body while repeating the positive affirmation out loud in order to more effectively trigger positive emotion. Practice incantation by waving your arms and smile while you are saying the positive affirmations and looking at the images. Believe in the words and images and say them with joy and determination.

For visualization you can utilize your vision book or board. For example, if you are desiring to travel to a certain destination for a vacation, find an exciting image of someone enjoying this destination in your vision book and hang it up where you can easily see it during your morning practice or hour of power.

Instead of memorizing your positive affirmations, print them out on paper so you can see them. Hang your positive affirmations next to your vision board.

Feel the emotions that the images and words bring to you as you repeat your positive affirmations (maybe three to seven times each) out loud while looking at your visualization images. Really imagine yourself enjoying that vacation destination or that new job. See yourself there as if you have already achieved it and are living it now. See yourself living it and, most importantly, feel how it feels to live it emotionally.

By offering new positive thoughts, affirmations, visualizations, and emotions in a daily morning practice you are reprogramming your brain to support the manifestation of your desires and your greatest potential for happiness!

See yourself there as if you have already achieved it and are living it now.

4.   **Physical Exercise.**

I spend at least 20 minutes engaging in some type of physical exercise. I vary it to include aerobics, resistance training and stretching/yoga. Recent studies have indicated that a minimum of 20 minutes of exercise daily is needed to stay healthy. Long sessions in the gym that can wear you out are not required to stay fit. And you don't have to join a gym or buy expensive equipment to start exercising. Even just walking at a brisk pace will go a long way toward building your fitness and staying healthy. Exercise can be at home or in the gym so there is no reason to put it off. Make it a daily habit and it will become a solid support for your health and happiness.

Exercise 1: Create Your Morning Practice

Make a special place in your home for quiet time. Though certain circumstances can make this challenging, try to find a place where you can be alone and help yourself with practices that support your well-being.

In your notebook or journal, map out your plan for your morning practice or hour of power. Make any notes you need to plan and create this empowering time of your day. What time will you start? Will your meditation be self-guided or guided? Do want to follow your breath or have a mantra? What sort of workouts do you plan to do? What sort of yoga or stretching will follow and from what source? Write out your positive affirmations and consider where you will source photos/pictures to hang up for your visualizations. What sorts of positive information will be part of your morning and from where will you source it? Consider what books you might read from and make a note to be sure to have a journal nearby for writing down what you are grateful for as well as new ideas for positive affirmations, dreams and desires.

Example:

1. Meditation – 20 min

2. Workout – 20 min

3. Yoga/stretching – positive affirmations/visualizations – reading and journaling – 20 min

Now, as we walk through a possible day, write down ideas for designing your life in a way that supports manifesting happiness. We will be putting it all together in the following chapter. This is the time to begin making notes and getting inspired!

Prepare for work

Before you leave for work or start your workday at home, put yourself in an extremely positive and empowered state. By utilizing the methods we have discussed earlier during your morning practice or hour of power, you will be ready to take on any challenges that come your way. In addition, make sure you are well groomed and dressed for success (and this means whatever success means to YOU – a great day at work or a beautiful walk in nature if you are retired, etc.)! Make sure you have everything prepared for your commute or have your home work space ready with your laptop and wireless networks set. By including a practice in your morning for empowering yourself and preparing ahead of time you can avoid negativity, distractions, and stress and instead remain positive, calm, and focused on your goals throughout your day.

If employed work is not part of your life you can still apply the skills in this section to the goals, appointments, chores, tasks, errands, projects, plans and challenges associated with your day.

Exercise 2: Prepare for your day

In your notebook or journal create a plan for preparing for your day that is unique to your circumstances and preferences. How can you create a prep plan that considers ways to block negativity and expand positivity? How about ways to empower yourself and stay stress-free?

The commute to work

If you're commuting and driving your own car, make sure you leave early enough so you don't have to rush to arrive on time. Putting pressure on yourself by speeding or rushing puts unneeded stress on you and can undo all the positive things you've done to start your day. Make sure you put your car keys in the same place every time, so you don't have to search frantically for them. Prepare a small backpack with water, a snack and reading material in case of traffic stalls. Make sure your cell phone is fully charged and you have a car charger in case of a weak battery.

Time your commute and give yourself an extra 30 minutes in case of delays. Additionally, find alternate routes in case of road blockages or closures. Given all your preplanning, be prepared in case of something extraordinary that can delay you.

Alternatively, if you are carpooling or taking public transportation make the same plans to be early to reduce stress.

Consider adding a positive audio experience to your commute such as pleasant, uplifting or calm, stress-reducing music. The time spent traveling between home and job is also a great time to listen to inspirational personal growth books or podcasts.

When unexpected traffic occurs or other stress-inducing events arise during your commute, use mindfulness for staying positive. Take a deep breath and let it out slowly paying attention to the feeling of your breath. Bring awareness into your hands and pay attention to the feeling of the steering wheel if you are driving. If you are a passenger pay attention to the feeling of your clothing material or something you may be holding. The point is to let go of thoughts and place your attention on perceiving where you are in the moment and what your senses are reporting to you. Refrain from judging and accept reality as it is in the moment, letting go of any need to control the situation. Using mindfulness in this way will help you maintain a calm and positive mind.

Exercise 3: Your commute or positive traveling time

In your notebook write down ideas for this time of day that will add to your positivity. What time will you be ready to go so there is no rushing or stress? How will you block negativity on your commute? What could you listen to while traveling that is positive? How could you practice mindfulness when traveling?

Arriving at your workplace

For arriving at work ready and confident, make a plan to be prepared for each workday the day before. Have your calendar up to date and make sure you have the resources you need to effectively perform your work tasks. Make sure all your tasks are completed like reports and other assignments you've been given. This way you can be sure to avoid stress and maintain a positive frame of mind.

Exercise 4: Arriving at your workplace

What can you do to improve the way you prepare for each day whether you are working or doing other things? How might you use planning and organizing to help you block negativity and expand positivity? Describe this in your notebook or journal.

Interacting with co-workers

As we discussed earlier, eliminate negative associations and people from your group if possible. Otherwise diminish their effect on you. For example, when people around you insert negativity into your environment, say, *Delete delete,* in your mind and follow it with doubling a positive word such as our favorite, *Dolphin, dolphin.* As mentioned before, this is an excellent tool for quickly blocking negativity and refocusing on the positive. Don't waste time gossiping or talking about trivial things or playing office politics. Focus on your tasks and be a team player. Be a leader and demonstrate positive qualities and a positive attitude to your co-workers. Aim for leaving each person you interact with feeling important and understood. Be an example of what you value most by striving to be positive, kind, compassionate, grateful, and joyful with others. As you strive to bring positivity to others, positivity will increase for you as well. Thus, interacting with your co-workers in a positive way is an essential component in staying focused on your goals and manifesting happiness!

Exercise 5: Interacting with co-workers/others

In your notebook or journal, create a plan for interacting for positivity with your co-workers or others in your life you encounter throughout your day. Are there most likely sources of negativity you can identify? What will you do if negativity arises? How will you block it? What can you do or say to block negativity and expand positivity?

Working – completing tasks

Be task oriented and accomplish your work projects in an efficient way. By setting a good example your team members will trust and admire you.

During your workday you will often be involved in activities and job tasks that are mundane and even boring. You must maintain your positivity by focusing on the bigger picture of what you are working for in your job. If you are employed by a large corporation, focus on the overall vision and mission of the company and how your job adds to that global vision for the company. A great example is a teller working in a bank. If the teller focuses on her specific job tasks it may not be very rewarding, but if she focuses on the overall mission of providing safety and security for the customers' money it becomes a higher purpose for her job.

Ideally, involve yourself only in activities that bring you happiness and joy. But when your work dictates that you must engage in tasks that are not of your choosing, reframe them in your mind so that you are focusing on how doing them will result in the best outcomes.

Letting your values of positivity and happiness direct your mindset when contributing in your work and tasks is a powerful way to stay balanced, calm and stress-free throughout your day.

Exercise 6: Completing tasks

In your notebook or journal, write about how you might apply these concepts to the way you work. Be aware of what thoughts you hold in your mind when completing tasks throughout your day. Are you focusing more often on thoughts that are negative, neutral, or positive? What thoughts can you plan to focus on to expand positivity?

Prioritizing and scheduling

In one of my past jobs, I was selected for an executive management position. The decision was based on my doing well in an independent management assessment conducted by a consulting firm. It involved lots of role playing, tests and measurements. One of the tests I went through was the "In Basket" assessment. This test was very powerful and taught me many lessons about prioritizing and scheduling my work. The test consisted of putting me in a room at a desk with an "In Basket" full of papers. I had 60 minutes to sort through the papers and schedule a number of tasks to see how efficient I could be. There were many memos from my 'boss' directing me to do a bunch of varied tasks. The one lesson I learned was to sort through all the memos first before scheduling anything. I found several memos in the bottom of the box that changed things I was supposed to do from earlier directions. So, by reading everything first, I saved a lot of time and completed all my tasks on time. This lesson was very valuable and helped me tremendously in my later career. Lesson learned: Avoid only a linear perspective in your work. Take a step back to take in the whole picture and create a plan for your approach to tasks. Whether you are taking things as they come one at a time or multi-tasking, take a breath to become mindful of the big picture which will allow you to prioritize and make conscious choices in your work, and to create solutions for staying efficient, stress-free, and positive.

Exercise 7: Prioritizing and scheduling

In your notebook or journal, write about how these ideas can be applied to the things you work on throughout your day.

Having lunch

The first and most important rule is that lunch must be away from work and in happy surroundings. If you sit most of the day for your work, consider taking a little walk to stretch your legs at lunchtime. Depending on your job or type of work, it could involve lunch with customers or just a short lunch break in your day. Regardless, avoid having lunch at your desk, work station or cubicle. The key reason is that you need to take a break from your surroundings and relax and enjoy your meal. Eating is a primary source of pleasure and you want to focus on it in a mindful way with no outside distractions. It's better to think of your work space as a place for work and eat in a different place where you can relax and not be interrupted or stressed out. Plus, it's important to refresh and recharge for the rest of your day!

Exercise 8: Your lunchtime

In your notebook or journal, write down some ideas for a lunch plan that expands positivity for you.

Attending meetings: stay on task and add positive comments

When in meetings, whether in person or remotely, stay focused on the discussion and make it a point to contribute your unique and valuable perspective by adding positive comments and constructive ideas whenever possible. If the meeting starts to take a negative downward spiral, refrain from joining in and instead stay solution focused letting your positive energy be a possibility for reversing the direction of the conversation and transforming the meeting.

Exercise 9: Attending meetings

In your notebook or journal: How can you can create and maintain positivity in your life when you are meeting with others?

In the classroom: sit up front to have more direct contact with the instructor

When in a classroom setting, consider sitting toward the front of the room where you can have more direct connection with the instructor while avoiding distractions that may occur in the back of the classroom. For greatest absorption of the knowledge being offered, practice listening with your whole body by turning your cell phone off, facing the teacher, keeping your body still, focusing on what is being said, and doing nothing other than listening.

Exercise 10: In the classroom

In your notebook or journal: How would you apply these ideas when you are learning something new? How could you maximize your experience and expand positivity while learning?

Reducing clutter and organizing

Reducing clutter and organizing your work and home environment aids in maintaining a clear, calm, and focused mind. A study conducted by the Princeton Neuroscience Institute supports the idea that having many things within your view while working results in those things competing with what you are trying to focus on. With disordered surroundings you may find yourself feeling distracted because your brain can't decide what to focus on. By organizing your work and living areas you are providing an optimal setting for staying positive and focused on your goals.

Reducing clutter and organizing is an important part of any environment we work or live in.

Exercise 11: Reducing clutter and organizing

In your notebook or journal, write about how you can reduce clutter and organize in your work space and in your living space. Create a plan for it.

The commute home:

The commute home is a great time to get some perspective on the day's events. Was there any time when you could have handled a situation in a more positive way? What went well today and what is there to be grateful for? Pay attention to the moment by following your breath for even just a few minutes of mindfulness to calm and restore serenity to your mind and heart. Then imagine what you will do and how positive you will feel upon arriving home. Imagine greeting family members or roommates with joyfulness, or, if you live alone, imagine feeling the happiness of arriving back into your personal space to begin an evening of self-care and enjoyment!

Exercise 12: The commute home

In your notebook or journal, write about your feelings and the transition from working on things in your day to arriving home. Reflect on moments of positivity and gratitude. How can you practice mindfulness as you travel home? How can you imagine sharing love and joy with others when you arrive home? How will you take care of yourself and enjoy the rest of your day?

Arriving home – Personal/Social/family/partner activities

When arriving home, it is important to leave your work-mind at work and be ready to focus on family members and pets in a positive and truly connected way.

Consider having screen-free quality time by putting your phone and computer social media and games away when visiting with loved ones at home.

To unwind, instead of alcohol, smoking, or computer/TV time, consider sitting outside or near a window for a bit to connect with nature; change into some comfortable clothes and do some stretching, do a short meditation to rebalance yourself, and/or take a walk to move your body, get some extra oxygen and stimulate your imagination for visualizing your goals.

Bring awareness to unplugging from technology and plugging into nature. Remember that you are a part of nature and separating from it for too long by being inside all day is not optimal for mood and health. Take time to fully connect by putting yourself in nature and connecting with the most beautiful source of positive energy and well-being to rejuvenate in mind, body, and spirit!

Exercise 13: Arriving home – Personal/Social/family/partner activities

In your notebook or journal, create a plan for expanding positivity when you arrive home. How will you focus on family members? How will you unplug and reconnect with nature? How will you fill your well and restore balance and energy?

Preparing to sleep – pre-sleep rituals and affirmations

Create a pre-sleep ritual that relaxes you and focuses on great sleep. I like to write down any things that are dominating my thoughts and place them in a notebook by my bed. I then say, "I'll work on these things tomorrow when I awaken."

I like to repeat my current affirmations and look at my vision book, so these positive thoughts, visuals and dreams are the most dominant things on my mind right before I fall asleep.

Exercise 14: Creating a pre-sleep ritual

In your notebook or journal, create a plan for your pre-sleep ritual. Where will you write your thoughts down? Where will you keep your positive affirmations? Where will you keep your vision book/board for viewing before turning out the lights?

The system is coming together! You have learned to block negativity, expand positivity, set goals, create positive affirmations, and design your day for positivity and happiness. In the next chapter you will be putting it all together to make this system your very own. It's time for practicing and mastering the skills you've learned for manifesting happiness to create your happy life!

Chapter Five Summary Points

1. Starting your day off right is the single most important thing you can do to ensure that you will have a happy day.

2. The Hour of Power (or shorter morning practice) is designed to connect your goals and values to your thoughts and actions for a great start to your day.

3. By including a ritual in your morning for empowering yourself and preparing ahead of time you can avoid negativity, distractions, and stress and instead remain positive, calm, and focused on your goals throughout your day.

4. Before you leave for work or start your workday at home, put yourself in an extremely positive and empowered state. By following the rituals we have discussed earlier during your hour of power, you will be ready to take on any challenges that come your way.

5. Ideally, involve yourself only in activities that bring you happiness and joy. But when your work dictates that you must engage in tasks that are not of your choosing, reframe them in your mind so that you are focusing on how doing them will result in the best outcomes.

6. Create a pre-sleep ritual that relaxes you and focuses on great sleep.

Chapter Six:

Manifesting Happiness - Putting It All Together

You must find the place inside yourself where nothing is impossible.

– Deepak Chopra

It's time to apply this system to your life for manifesting happiness!

To bring it all together, we are empowered with our skills for blocking negativity and expanding positivity so let's start with understanding our basic values and beliefs. Let's use the principles of our happiness system to complete a values assessment and create a plan to follow to achieve greater happiness in our life.

Performing a values assessment:

We'll start by picking the area of finance from our eight-sided overlapping wheel of values. Our premise of aiming for our happiest life overall assumes that we achieve high levels of happiness and satisfaction by maximizing our potential in each area of the wheel.

Step one is to eliminate the negative influences in our financial life. Let's examine our current financial situation. Make a real assessment and ask questions like: *Do I suffer, worry and stress from any aspect of my finances? Am I in debt, behind on payments, overextended? Am I earning enough money to live a good life? Do I have assets and savings and generate more earnings than I spend? Is there someone in my life who is draining money from me?* These questions must be answered, and the negative habits, influences of the people involved need to be eliminated or minimized.

A good way to examine our current financial status is to create a budget and see exactly where we stand. Let's keep it simple – it really doesn't need to be complicated to be effective. Write down and calculate all the money that comes in from all sources on a monthly basis and then, in a separate list, write down all of your expenses and things you spend money on every month. Now subtract your expenses from your income. Do you have money left over or are you short every month? If you have money left over, open a savings account and deposit that money into it monthly. Once you have enough in savings, start a simple investment program to make your money grow. However, if you are short every month, you may be either using your credit cards, borrowing money or selling things to cover the shortfall. This can be stressful and can ultimately lead to more worries and problems.

If you are in debt, there are two basic ways to solve the problem. You can examine your expenses carefully and eliminate the unnecessary expenses or you can find a way to make more money. Why not do both things? Step One of our system calls for eliminating all negative influences concerning our finances. Go ahead and eliminate all unnecessary expenses first and then let's be proactive and use the next step of our system, our E+R=O formula. In this case E= too much debt and unnecessary spending.

R= how we react or respond to the situation. Do we realize that our situation is totally in our control and can be fixed by changing our thinking and our actions? A positive reaction R is to make a budget and then carefully eliminate all non-essential expenses. For example, buying $6.00 lattes and small compulsive purchases is money wasted. Go over your spending habits and reduce all expenses to just cover your fixed expenses and then add back in a few things if they fit.

So now your O or outcome is you are controlling your spending and you have created a better, more positive financial environment.

The next step of our system is Goal Setting. Now we can create a plan to get out of debt, make more money and have more options for ourselves. Go through the SMART goal-setting process to create some powerful financial goals. Specific, Measurable, Attainable, Relevant and

Timely. For example: *I will save 10% of my income every month and open a separate bank savings account to deposit the money in for safe keeping.*

You might want to make some additional goals to acquire things you want like a new car, house or vacation.

The next step is to create powerful affirmations to support your goals and to visualize them daily. For example: *I am totally in control of my finances* or *I am so happy and grateful that I have a savings account and that I am adding to it regularly.* Refer back to Chapter Four on how to best create powerful affirmations.

Now visualize the attainment of your goal and feel the positive emotions relating to how proud you are for reaching your goal.

You can create additional goals for things that you want or need following the same process outlined above. Make a vision board and add the outcomes you want to it. You will be learning about vision books/boards in Exercise 2 of this chapter.

In summary, eliminate the negatives, focus on a positive plan, take full responsibility for your situation and make changes. Create goals and affirmations and visualize the manifestation of those goals. You are the creator of your future!

Exercise 1: Values Assessment

To create a comprehensive life plan, review each of the eight value areas and put together an assessment and plan like the one above so you are focusing on all of the eight wellness areas of your life. Remember to take each category and rate your satisfaction in each area on a scale from one to ten, one being totally unsatisfactory and ten being highly satisfactory. The categories with example ratings are:

Spiritual – rating 7

Financial – rating 3

Physical – rating 7

Emotional – rating 5

Environmental – rating 6

Occupational – rating 9

Social – rating 9

Intellectual – rating 9

Given these example ratings, it looks like some work is needed in four areas and some serious work in one of them. We take the categories that are lacking, repeat the process explained above, and make goals and create positive affirmations to bring them up to better levels. Take this time to do some writing and apply this process to your eight wellness areas of your life.

Exercise 2: Create a Vision Book/Board

This can be as simple or elaborate as you want it to be. Here's what I do.

1. Purchase a large loose-leaf notebook with plastic sheets so that you can slip in pictures and sheets of paper for each of your goals.

2. Review each goal you have and find or make an image that best represents the achievement of that specific goal. For example, to have a picture of your savings goal use one of your bank statements and write in the amount you want to have in your account. If you want $10,000 in your account just mark out your current balance and put $10,000 on that line. If you want a better, fitter body, find a photo of someone you want to look like from a fitness magazine and put your picture on their head or just remove their head and write your name on the picture. If you want a new car, go to the dealer and test drive the one you want. Get a brochure on that exact car and put its picture in your book.

3. Make one page for each goal in the notebook with the image you have chosen—use a plastic separator sheet so you can place the image in the notebook where it can be seen easily. Divide the sheets into categories for each of your current goals. You should have a minimum of eight separate goals for each area in your life.

4. Look at each page daily and visualize having obtained your goal—be grateful that you have achieved it and evoke the emotions you will have when it's yours.

5. Believe that your thoughts are things and that your goals are materializing by the law of attraction and the laws of quantum physics. The full power of the universe is lining up to fulfill your dreams.

6. Review your goal book every morning and every night before sleeping to reinforce your burning desire to achieve them.

It's that easy to make and it is one of the most powerful tools to help you focus your visualization efforts on your goals.

Use the values assessment, goal-setting exercise, affirmations and vision board to make positive changes in your life and become empowered with a positive plan for your life and your happiness!

Putting It All Together!

To continue on your journey, it's important to review the new skills that you have learned and to incorporate them into your daily plan.

By now you have learned that happiness is a choice you can make and that you have a set of tools to create the happiness you truly want for yourself in your life.

You have learned to block negativity from negative news and other people as well as from negative thoughts and self-talk. You have learned to expand positivity with thoughts and words of your choosing or with my technique of *delete, delete* then *dolphin, dolphin.*

You have also learned that you can change the outcome of any situation by simply changing your response to events that occur in different situations using the formula E + R = O. You have learned that you have a choice in creating the outcome of any situation.

You are never powerless and always powerful!

You have learned to set goals and create positive affirmations to achieve anything you desire in your life. It's important to control your life by creating a positive plan. By creating a positive plan that you can execute and follow every day, you control your day. By following this plan, you can ensure your happiness on a daily basis and throughout your life.

You have created a vision book that contains visual examples of all the goals that you're seeking to achieve. By reviewing your vision book every day in the morning and evening you're able to continually reinforce the manifestation of the positive things you want in your life.

You have learned to create daily practices to program your mind for happiness and success, things like using the morning hour of power, or even a morning practice that is a shorter time period, that you take just for yourself to create a positive day. Starting out this way continues to reinforce that you are in charge of your day, your beliefs, your feelings and your happiness.

You have learned to relieve stress to be healthy and happy. One of the great things that you will master will be how to meditate. Meditating on a daily basis is one of the best ways to relieve stress. Meditation also puts you in touch with your inner self and is the best way to prepare for visualizing achieving all your goals.

You've learned how to plan your day to reduce stress in different types of situations. You've learned to prepare yourself in the morning to start out with a positive attitude and keep that attitude going under different circumstances that occur during your day.

Now is the time to engage your values and incorporate all these new skills into your day to truly manifest happiness in your life. Ending your day positively is just as important as starting your day on a positive note.

The last thing to do before going to sleep is to say your affirmations and review your goals and the actions you took to advance yourself toward the achievement of those goals. Start by reviewing your goals and looking at the images in your vision book/board. Visualize that you are manifesting those images and goals and be sure that you are incorporating all the good feelings you have evoked by imagining achieving them.

Be sure to also write down all the things that you are currently thinking about that might make sleeping difficult. Writing down a list of everything you're considering or thinking about before you go to sleep which will help you have a deeper and more relaxed sleep time. After recording all your thoughts of the next day, simply say that you are finished with these items and you will work on them tomorrow.

Be sure to review the positive experiences you had during your day and know that they can manifest again the next day. You have the ability now to have good days every day!

Keep in mind that happiness comes from within and is not created by external things or other people in your world. Happiness is there inside you all the time waiting for your attention. Let it light up your path today as you pursue your dreams. Complete your plan, focus on your vision, and believe in yourself. You truly are powerful. Use all the tools you have learned to create your best life. You are totally in control of your happiness!

Thank you for your time in joining me here in these pages. May abundance in all areas of life be yours. Now go forth and block negativity, expand positivity and manifest happiness in your life!

Chapter Six Summary Points:

1. Let's use the principles of our happiness system to complete a values assessment and create a plan to follow to achieve greater happiness in our life.

2. Eliminate the negatives, focus on a positive plan, take full responsibility for your situation and make changes. Create goals and affirmations and visualize the manifestation of those goals. You are the creator of your future!

3. Create a vision board or book. Review your goal book every morning and every night before sleeping to reinforce your burning desires to achieve them.

4. Be sure to review the positive experiences you had during your day and know that they can manifest again the next day. You have the ability now to have good days every day.

5. Keep in mind that happiness comes from within and is not created by external things or other people in your world. Happiness is there inside you all the time waiting for your attention. Let it light up your path today as you pursue your dreams. Complete your plan, focus on your vision, and believe in yourself. You truly are powerful. Use all the tools you have learned to create your best life. You are totally in control of your happiness!

Appendix:

I. Summary of Our System:

* Block negativity from sources such as negative news, negativity from others, and negative thoughts and self-talk

* Expand positivity in ways such as reprogramming the mind for positivity, strengthening the brain with meditation, and practicing gratitude

* Set goals based on your values and dreams

* Create positive affirmations for making the goals you set a reality

* Design your life with visualization and create a vision book or board

* Put it all together for a daily system of manifesting happiness for life

II. Exercises Catalog:

All your exercises in one group for regular use as you continue to design your life and manifest happiness.

Exercises by chapter:

Chapter One:

Exercise 1: Blocking Negative Sensationalized News Sources and Replacing Them with Neutral or Positive Information

Make a list of all your information sources.

In your notebook or journal record all the sources of news and information that you are affected by every day. Start out with what happens as soon as you arise from sleep in the morning. Are you awakened by the radio alarm? What are the radio disc jockeys talking about? Do you listen to radio or TV while having breakfast or when getting dressed? The aim here is to become more conscious of when you read, listen or watch mass media. Additionally, what are you doing on the computer or phone that may be affecting your thoughts? Considering all the information your mind is exposed to each day, which is negative? Neutral? Positive?

Example:

LIST OF NEWS SOURCES:

1.   Radio alarm with talk radio station
2.   MSN browser page
3.   News apps
4.   Twitter
5.   Facebook
6.   Instagram
7.   Email subscriptions
8.   USA Today
9.   CNN
10.   FOX
11.   Gossip

The point of the exercise is to monitor all information sources of negativity that are entering your conscious mind and then block them.

By monitoring, we have the ability to raise our awareness of what our mind is being exposed to and to block incoming negative information that causes harmful programming. Paying attention to negative information leads to negative thoughts, which in turn leads to negative feelings. By eliminating the negative we make way for the positive.

Record all the sources for one week and then review and eliminate all the negative sources and replace them with either neutral or positive sources of information. Some examples of good sources of positive information or positive programming are positive news, neutral sources of news (these provide brief headlines without sensationalized information), self-help, inspirational music, fiction, poetry or other forms of art, learning a new skill, personal and professional development, and biographies.

Monitor yourself after blocking the negative input and see how differently you feel in general, about yourself and about the world around you.

Exercise 2: Adopting a Phrase to Say in Your Mind to Counteract the Effects of Negativity

Choose a phrase to say each time you are exposed to negativity such as bad news, violence, a depressing story, unkindness from others, or negative thoughts and self-talk. The phrase can be something like, "I reject this," "Cancel, cancel," or, "I'm envisioning a world that is kind, helpful, and happy." The phrase can become a mantra or affirmation you say each time negativity arises in your environment. Try this for a week every time any form of negativity arises and consider the difference it makes in how you feel.

Exercise 3: Negative to Positive Mindfulness Tool

Sometimes negative thoughts can feel stuck in our mind. The thoughts keep churning around repeating themselves and we feel unable to get them out of our head. We can train our mind so that we gain control over the quality of our thoughts. This exercise provides a skill for doing this.

A strategy to stop negative recurring thoughts is Negative to Positive Mindfulness.

When a negative thought gets stuck in your mind and is affecting your mood in a negative way, you can use the Negative to Positive

Mindfulness Tool as a strategy to let go of the thought and produce a positive thought that will improve how you feel. Here's how you do it:

Find your breath—and by this, I mean actually feel where the wind of your breath is on your mouth or nose when breathing a natural breath. Then take the negative thought and visualize it floating away—far away. Then turn your attention back to your breath for just one breath in which you again note the sensation of the wind of your breath. Now you have successfully anchored your mind in the present moment and released the negative thought. From here you can generate a positive thought, which will provide positive feelings. One of the easiest ways to generate a positive thought is to think of something for which you are grateful. As you visualize this, let the positive feeling of gratitude wash over you. Having successfully released the negative thought you can move forward with your day with a positive mind and feeling good.

Chapter Two:

Exercise 1: Considering Positivity When Encountering Negativity

When negativity arises, whether from the news, other people, or from your own thoughts or self-talk, ask yourself, *What am I thinking and feeling right now?* Then ask, *What do I want to be thinking and feeling?* Ask yourself the questions, *If I was in a happy state of mind how would I be thinking and how would I be feeling about this situation? How would I be looking at the bright side? How would I be solution focused? In what ways would I be optimistic? How would I find value in this situation?*

Then find something positive to focus on. Focus on this positive thing—it could be something you're grateful for. Feel into how this positive thing makes you feel. You are basically telling your mind, *This is how I'm going to think and feel right now.*

This is teaching your mind that you are in control of thoughts and feelings. This is a skill that can be practiced and mastered. The brain adapts and the mind will learn that you are in charge of what thoughts serve you and what thoughts do not. The mind will become flexible and open to your direction. You will be able to let go of the negative easily and refocus the mind on something positive. In doing so you will be creating good feelings within you at will.

Exercise 2: Envisioning a Positive Day

Envision yourself living out the day thinking in a positive way and feeling the way you want to feel. How do you respond to feeling tired when you wake up in the morning? How do you respond to conflict or something not going your way with work? Imagining yourself living out the day and taking control of your thoughts by focusing on the positive in every situation, and thus controlling how you feel, teaches your mind how it will behave.

Remind yourself regularly, *When I have this or that problem, I will respond in this or that way because I am 100% responsible for my happiness.* You are in charge—not your mind.

Whether negativity is coming from the environment, such as the news or other people, or from your own thoughts or self-talk, it is important to block it and refocus on positivity.

Exercise 3: Positive Words After Blocking Negativity

In Chapter 1, Exercise 2 we discussed utilizing a phrase when negativity arises. This exercise adds to that by offering some specific and powerful words that quickly transform negativity to positivity.

As soon as negativity comes at you in any way, say the words out loud or in your mind, *Delete, delete.* Then follow it up with a positive word, mantra, or affirmation of your choice. I love the word "dolphin" because dolphins are a symbol of happiness and kindness. You could consider saying, *Delete, delete,* and then follow it up with, *dolphin, dolphin,* to turn the mind from negative to positive in an instant. And if saying, *Dolphin, dolphin,* sounds kind of silly then all the better. Keep it fun and positive and watch your thinking and mood brighten up instantaneously!

Exercise 4: Practicing Gratitude

Gratitude is an excellent way of practicing positivity. Thinking of things for which you are thankful not only creates positive feelings within you in the present moment, it also magnifies positive emotions. Practicing gratitude on a regular basis trains your mind to stay focused on what you appreciate, which expands the positivity you experience.

1.To get started, make a list of things for which you are grateful. Now get a jar or a box and label it "Gratitude". Put this list in your Gratitude jar/box. Whenever you think of something you are thankful for add it to this container. At times when you are feeling down, take out some of the notes to remind yourself of what there is to be thankful for.

2.Each morning, imagine three things for which you are grateful. Let the feeling of thankfulness wash over you as you visualize– really feel into the positive emotions that arise.

3.At night, before going to sleep, write down in a gratitude journal three things for which you are grateful. This puts your mind in a positive state before sleeping.

4.Write gratitude letters to people who made a difference in your life. Because you matter, when the recipients of your letters hear from you that you are thankful for how they touched your life, you will have created positivity for them as well as yourself.

5. Look around you, wherever you are (you can do this throughout the day) and look for things or situations you appreciate. When you notice something you do not appreciate, practice ignoring it rather than staying focused on it and judging it as negative. Then redirect your focus to looking for what you do appreciate. This trains your mind to focus only on what you appreciate.

6. Find or purchase a rock that you like. Keep it in a place in your environment where you will see it often. Each time you notice the rock, touch it and think of something for which you are grateful. This keeps the positivity flowing all day!

Exercise 5: Meditation

12 Benefits of Meditation

1. Strengthens your mind
2. Improves your ability to pay attention and stay focused
3. Decreases your capacity to feel emotional and physical pain
4. Broadens your perspective
5. Aids in managing your emotions (anger, aggression, greed, jealousy, fear, anxiety)
6. Training in meditation is about mastering your mind so that you can take control of your emotions and painful thoughts and not be consumed by them
7. Aids you in feeling more emotionally balanced
8. Through meditation you learn that moods, emotions, and negative character traits are temporary and changeable
9. Improves your relationships
10. Increases and deepens your experience of positive emotions such as love, inner peace, confidence, generosity, inspiration, contentment, awe, joy, and altruistic kindness
11. Research has shown that with as few as eight sessions of meditation, meditators rated themselves an average of 20% happier and had improved immune system responsiveness
12. Meditation has been shown to cause an increase in the brain's grey-matter density in parts of the brain associated with memory, compassion, self-awareness, and introspection

Goals of Meditation

- The goal of meditation is to transform the mind from weak to strong. This happens because when we hold our attention in the present moment for extended amounts of time (5 min, 10 min, 20 min, etc.), as we do when we meditate, it strengthens the mind so that we have more control of our thoughts and thus emotions.

- The aim in meditation is to anchor our attention in the present moment through focusing on the breath, and when thoughts arise (or the mind wanders), avoiding judging the thoughts and instead remaining emotionally unattached toward the thoughts, and then letting the thoughts go and gently returning our attention to the breath.

- A big misconception about meditation is that we are supposed to blank out our mind and have no thoughts. However, the goal of meditation is not to have no thoughts, it is to let go of thoughts as they arise and then return our focus to the present moment.

- With meditation we are aiming to train the mind for increased awareness, to remain calm and balanced and to more deeply engage in the present moment.

How to Meditate

Find a quiet comfortable place to sit. It can be in a chair with your feet flat on the ground or on the floor with legs crossed in front.

It helps to keep your spine straight, but your jaw, neck and shoulders relaxed. A good way to do this is to imagine a piece of string pulling you up from the top of your head while all tension leaves the rest of your body.

Your hands can be in a relaxed position on your knees or in your lap. Eyes may be closed or open partially.

Sitting in a state of receptivity with a small smile on your lips, you welcome all inner and outer experiences as they come into your awareness. In this way you are practicing being open and accepting of reality – not judgmental (even if it's a disturbance such as a car horn or dog barking).

Pay attention to the sensation of your breath going in and out of your nostrils. Let your mind rest in the physical sensation of inhalation and then exhalation. You may choose to focus on the rise and fall of your chest or belly. Just breath naturally and be present with your breath.

When your mind wanders, notice the thought with nonjudgmental kindness. Consider that your mind is just doing what it naturally does – shows you pictures. Then gently redirect your attention back to your breath.

If there is a thought that keeps resurfacing or you find it challenging to redirect your attention back to your breath, imagine letting the thought go on a cloud or giving the thought to a friendly dolphin that swims away with it.

Stay with this process of following the breath and letting go of thoughts until it's time to end the meditation.

Try to meditate each day for a minimum of 20 -30 minutes for the greatest benefits. If your time is limited try meditating in small increments throughout your day - 5 minutes here, 10 minutes there, etc.

Exercise 6: Creating Positive Habits

This exercise asks you to start thinking about positivity as part of your daily and weekly plan. We will be building an ultimate plan in Chapter 6. For now, start to consider how practicing positivity can fit into your life for manifesting happiness. Here are three possibilities:

#1. Start the day with a morning practice that gets you focused on positivity and feeling emotionally balanced. This can include body-mind connection practices such as meditation, stretching, yoga, and exercise. Journaling goals and gratitude as well as exposing your mind to positive sources of information that are inspiring and uplifting are some other ways to start your day in a positive way.

#2. Before you go to sleep at night, imagine yourself succeeding in having the happy life you want to have. Imagine yourself thinking the way you want to think and feeling the way you want to feel.

#3. If you know ahead of time that a challenging situation is coming up then consider rehearsing ahead of time how you will think and feel in the situation.

Chapter Three:

Exercise 1: Value Identification

Let's spend some time identifying our values which will make the goal-setting process much more powerful. You may find you have current values as well as ideal values. Take a look at the following list.

Freedom	Safety
Friends	Security
Family	Confidence
Career	Relaxation
Church	Religion
School	Relationships
Education	Charity
Action	Communication
Fitness	Privacy
Health	Community
Country	Sports
Associations	Clubs
Love	Learning
Travel	

Consider each idea separately and explore your beliefs related to that concept as it pertains to your life. Take some time to write about your beliefs and what you value most. What are your beliefs regarding each of these areas? How much importance and priority do you assign to each area? How do you value each area currently? How would you value each area ideally? What do you envision in each of these areas for creating your most happy life?

Now let's look at eight areas of life that affect our wellness. They are:

Spiritual

Financial

Physical

Emotional

Environmental

Occupational

Social

Intellectual

Now consider your values and beliefs in each of the eight wellness areas of your life. Rate your happiness from 1–10 in each of the eight areas. This will provide you with a guide to areas that you want to improve and give you tangible things to focus on achieving.

Here is an example of goal-oriented activities in each wellness area that takes into consideration values and beliefs:

Spiritual - Perform a morning meditation for 20 minutes

Financial - Open an IRA and contribute monthly

Physical - Go for 30-minute walk daily and do 15 minutes of weight bearing exercises

Emotional - Make a weekly date with your significant other

Environment - Create a goal to find a new home that better fits your needs

Occupational - Develop a better relationship with your supervisor at work

Social - Strengthen your personal relationships

Intellectual - Read a new book every month that adds knowledge to your passion

Exercise 2: Setting a SMART Goal

SMART Goal: Specific, Measurable, Achievable, Relevant and Time-bound

Example:

I will set an alarm for 5:30 AM and wake up 30 minutes early each morning starting tomorrow morning, February 21, 2019. I will dress in comfortable clothes and sit in a quiet place and meditate for 20 minutes. After meditation, I will read and focus on my current goals and affirmations before starting my day.

Practice by writing down one SMART goal for yourself.

Once the goal is set, we must make it real. We must write it down and read it every morning and every evening before we go to sleep. We must visualize it, create a picture of it and post it where we can see it every day. Share the goal with a friend and concentrate on the feelings and emotions of achieving it. I recently had a goal of selling a condo that I owned. I printed out a copy of the listing and wrote *sold* across it and put it on my refrigerator in my kitchen. I saw it daily and focused on the sale. It sold in three weeks for a good price!

Write down goals for each of the eight wellness areas of your life.

Chapter Four:

Exercise 1: Creating Your Own Positive Affirmations

Begin making a list of positive affirmations that go with each of the goals you are creating in the eight wellness areas of your life. Make sure each of your affirmations contain all three components that define an effective positive affirmation. You will be expanding on this in Chapter Six, but you can begin now.

Exercise 2: Saying and Writing Your Positive Affirmations

Say your positive affirmations out loud to yourself when your brain is in an alpha state such as in the morning when you first wake up, while meditating or praying, and at night before falling asleep. It is also helpful to write down each positive affirmation at least once daily in your journal.

Chapter Five:

Exercise 1: Create Your Morning Practice

Make a special place in your home for quiet time. Though certain circumstances can make this challenging, try to find a place where you can be alone and help yourself with practices that support your well-being.

In your notebook or journal, map out your plan for your morning practice or hour of power. Make any notes you need to plan and create this empowering time of your day. What time will you start? Will your meditation be self-guided or guided? Do want to follow your breath or have a mantra? What sort of workouts do you plan to do? What sort of yoga or stretching will follow and from what source? Write out your positive affirmations and consider where you will source photos/pictures to hang up for your visualizations. What sorts of positive information will be part of your morning and from where will you source it? Consider what books you might read from and make a note to be sure to have a journal nearby for writing down what you are grateful for as well as new ideas for positive affirmations, dreams and desires.

Example:

1. Meditation – 20 min
2. Workout – 20 min
3. Yoga/stretching – positive affirmations/visualizations – reading and journaling – 20 min

Exercise 2: Prepare for your day

In your notebook or journal create a plan for preparing for your day that is unique to your circumstances and preferences. How can you create a prep plan that considers ways to block negativity and expand positivity? How about ways to empower yourself and stay stress-free?

Exercise 3: Your commute or positive traveling time

In your notebook write down ideas for this time of day that will add to your positivity. What time will you be ready to go so there is no rushing or stress? How will you block negativity on your commute? What could you listen to while traveling that is positive? How could you practice mindfulness when traveling?

Exercise 4: Arriving at your workplace

What can you do to improve the way you prepare for each day whether you are working or doing other things? How might you use planning and organizing to help you block negativity and expand positivity? Describe this in your notebook or journal.

Exercise 5: Interacting with co-workers/others

In your notebook or journal, create a plan for interacting for positivity with your co-workers or others in your life you encounter throughout your day. Are there most likely sources of negativity you can identify? What will you do if negativity arises? How will you block it? What can you do or say to block negativity and expand positivity?

Exercise 6: Completing tasks

In your notebook or journal, write about how you might apply these concepts to the way you work. Be aware of what thoughts you hold in your mind when completing tasks throughout your day. Are you focusing more often on thoughts that are negative, neutral, or positive? What thoughts can you plan to focus on to expand positivity?

Exercise 7: Prioritizing and scheduling

In your notebook or journal, write about how these ideas can be applied to the things you work on throughout your day.

Exercise 8: Your lunchtime

In your notebook or journal, write down some ideas for a lunch plan that expands positivity for you.

Exercise 9: Attending meetings

In your notebook or journal: How can you can create and maintain positivity in your life when you are meeting with others?

Exercise 10: In the classroom

In your notebook or journal: How would you apply these ideas when you are learning something new? How could you maximize your experience and expand positivity while learning?

Exercise 11: Reducing clutter and organizing

In your notebook or journal, write about how you can reduce clutter and organize in your work space and in your living space. Create a plan for it.

Exercise 12: The commute home

In your notebook or journal, write about your feelings and the transition from working on things in your day to arriving home. Reflect on moments of positivity and gratitude. How can you practice mindfulness as you travel home? How can you imagine sharing love and joy with others when you arrive home? How will you take care of yourself and enjoy the rest of your day?

Exercise 13: Arriving home – Personal/Social/family/partner activities

In your notebook or journal, create a plan for expanding positivity when you arrive home. How will you focus on family members? How will you unplug and reconnect with nature? How will you fill your well and restore balance and energy?

Exercise 14: Creating a pre-sleep ritual

In your notebook or journal, create a plan for your pre-sleep ritual. Where will you write your thoughts down? Where will you keep your positive affirmations? Where will you keep your vision book/board for viewing before turning out the lights?

Chapter Six:

Exercise 1: Values Assessment

To create a comprehensive life plan, review each of the eight value areas and put together an assessment and plan like the one above so you are focusing on all of the eight wellness areas of your life. I like to take each category and rate my satisfaction in each area on a scale from one to ten, one being totally unsatisfactory and ten being highly satisfactory. The categories with example ratings are:

Spiritual – rating 7

Financial – rating 3

Physical – rating 7

Emotional – rating 5

Environmental – rating 6

Occupational – rating 9

Social – rating 9

Intellectual – rating 9

Given these example ratings, it looks like some work is needed in four areas and some serious work in one of them. We take the categories that are lacking, repeat the process explained above, and make goals and create positive affirmations to bring them up to better levels. Take this time to do some writing and apply this process to your eight wellness areas of your life.

Exercise 2: Create a Vision Book/Board

This can be as simple or elaborate as you want it to be. Here's what I do.

1.   Purchase a large loose-leaf notebook with plastic sheets so that you can slip in pictures and sheets of paper for each of your goals.

2.   Review each goal you have and find or make an image that best represents the achievement of that specific goal. For example, to have a picture of your savings goal use one of your bank statements and write in the amount you want to have in your account. If you want $10,000 in your account just mark out your current balance and put $10,000 on that line. If you want a better, fitter body, find a photo of someone you want to look like from a fitness magazine and put your picture on their head or just remove their head and write your name on the picture. If you want a new car, go to the dealer and test drive the one you want. Get a brochure on that exact car and put its picture in your book.

3.   Make one page for each goal in the notebook with the image you have chosen—use a plastic separator sheet so you can place the image in the notebook where it can be seen easily. Divide the sheets into categories for each of your current goals. You should have a minimum of eight separate goals for each area in your life.

4.   Look at each page daily and visualize having obtained your goal—be grateful that you have achieved it and evoke the emotions you will have when it's yours!

5.   Believe that your thoughts are things and that your goals are materializing by the law of attraction and the laws of quantum physics. The full power of the universe is lining up to fulfill your dreams.

6.   Review your goal book every morning and every night before sleeping to reinforce your burning desire to achieve them.

It's that easy to make and it is one of the most powerful tools to help you focus your visualization efforts on your goals.

Use the values assessment, goal-setting exercise, affirmations and vision board to make positive changes in your life and become empowered with a positive plan for your life and your happiness!

III. Inspirational Readings

The Seven Spiritual Laws of Success, Deepak Chopra

The Success Principles, Jack Canfield

Think and Grow Rich, Napoleon Hill

The Code of the Extraordinary Mind, Vishen Lakhiani

The Biology of Belief, Bruce Lipton

Mind to Matter, Dawson Church

Inner Engineering, Sadguru Jaggi Vasudev

Infinite Possibilities, Mike Dooley

High Performance Habits, Brendon Burchard

Becoming Supernatural, Dr. Joe Dispenza

Awaken the Giant Within, Tony Robbins

This book will change the way you think, feel and experience reality. Specialists in health, success, positivity and happiness, Dr. Logan Chamberlain and Dr. Jacquelyn Somach team up to bring you a powerful system for transforming your life. How to Manifest Happiness lays out a clear path with skills and exercises to design and shape a personal plan that will have you manifesting happiness -today!

Take control of your feelings, your future and your happiness by learning to:

Train your mind, Block negativity, Expand positivity,

Set SMART goals, Utilize positive affirmations, Live more consciously

Respond instead of reacting, Practice gratitude, Meditate,

Create a vision board/book and Design your life.

Please visit www.howtomanifesthappiness.com for more information.

Author Biographies:

Dr. Logan Chamberlain received his master's degree from Texas A&M University in Clinical Psychology and his Ph.D. from Colorado State University in Human Resource Development. Dr. Chamberlain is an entrepreneur, author and consultant. He received the distinguished honor alumnus award from Colorado State University in 2002. Dr. Chamberlain is exceptionally passionate about helping others to take control of their happiness!

Dr. Jacquelyn Somach received her Ph.D. from Pacifica Graduate Institute in Clinical Psychology and is a licensed mental health counselor with a private practice in Venice, Florida. Dr. Somach specializes in positive psychology and the science of well-being with the goal of empowering individuals with the principles, skills and practices for realizing their greatest potential for happiness!

www.ingramcontent.com/pod-product-compliance
Lightning Source LLC
Chambersburg PA
CBHW022122280326
41933CB00007B/510